W9-CSY-990

Introduction

If any one man may be said to control a hockey game, it is the center. He is the team general. Each game starts with a face-off. The puck is dropped between the two opposing centers, who battle for it with their sticks and their bodies. For this reason centers have to be strong and are usually the best stickhandlers on a team. There can be as many as fifty face-offs during a game. Most of them are taken by the centers.

This is the story of Phil Esposito, center for the Boston Bruins, who has the hottest stick in hockey. He is big and strong. Phil sets up plays in face-offs and is a team leader. His main job for the fighting Boston club is to score goals. He does it better than any player in the game today.

When Phil skates within 20 feet of the net, where the action is the heaviest, opposing goaltenders are filled with terror. He is strong enough to fight off players who get in his way, and Esposito's lightning-fast wrist shot has made him hockey's all-time high scorer.

Sports Hero

Phil Esposito

by Marshall and Sue Burchard

G. P. Putnam's Sons • **New York**

PHOTO CREDITS

Sault *Daily Star,* pp. 6, 9, 15
Mrs. Marie Dagg, pp. 18, 19, 20
Phil Esposito Management Corporation, pp. 2, 56, 72
United Press International, pp. 26, 31, 34, 37, 40, 42, 44,
  47, 49, 51, 56, 58, 61, 62, 65, 66, 69, 70, 72, 76, 80,
  86, 88, 93

Contents

Every day many big freighters pass through
the canals in Phil Esposito's hometown,
Sault Ste. Marie.

1

The Land of Hockey

The city of Sault Ste. Marie, On-
tario, is famous for its shipping can-
als and for being the birthplace of
Phil Esposito and his brother, Tony.
Sault Ste. Marie, called the Soo for
short, lies on the north shore of the
St. Marys River on the border of
Canada and the United States. On the
south shore sits its U.S. twin city,
Sault Ste. Marie, Michigan.

As in most Canadian towns, the biggest sport is hockey. Nearly every boy dreams of being a professional hockey player, and nearly every boy begins skating before he starts school.

Phil Esposito was born on April 23, 1943. He weighed eleven pounds. Tony was born a year later.

Phil was such a big awkward child that he was slow learning to walk. But by the time he was four years old he had his first pair of skates.

Pat Esposito did not have much time to play with his sons. He had two jobs. He worked as a foreman for the Algoma Mines, and he was a part-time welder.

But he always made sure his boys had a place to skate. He flooded the backyard until a sheet of ice, about twenty by thirty feet, had formed. Then he sent Phil and Tony out to play on it. He built a net for Tony, who liked playing goal.

The Algoma Mines factory, where Mr. Esposito worked as a foreman.

When Tony wanted to skate around shooting the puck, the boys would call their mother. Frances Esposito couldn't skate, but she spent hours standing in the nets trying to stop the pucks that came shooting over the ice.

Hockey soon became the most important interest in Phil's life. When he came home from school at three, he would skate until five thirty. He didn't spend much time on homework, so he didn't make very good grades. When he came in for supper, he didn't even take off his skates. After supper he went out and played until it was so dark he couldn't see.

In the spring the Soo boys traded their skates for shoes and played street hockey. Phil went through four pairs of shoes over the summer.

Every day during the long Canadian winters Phil and his friends played hockey. Then on Saturday night they would listen to a real game. There was no television, but Phil didn't need a picture of the action. He could see it all clearly in his mind.

2

Climbing the Hockey Ladder

Phil was thirteen years old when he tried out for his first team, the Algoma Contractors. It was sponsored for boys his age by the mining company where Phil's father worked.

About sixty boys tried out. The tryouts were held outdoors and lasted several days. The boys began skating at nine in the morning and stopped at six at night. Sometimes the temperature dropped to 25 degrees below zero with a strong wind blowing.

All Phil could think about was making the team. He knew he could handle the stick well. But because he was so big, he was a little slow on the ice and had trouble getting the puck. When Coach Angelo Bombacco picked his team, he did not call the name Esposito. Phil went back to the dressing room and burst into tears.

The next year Phil made the Contractors, but he still had trouble with his size. He lacked coordination. Coach Bombacco took him to see a doctor who suggested some exercises to help.

Phil's biggest problem was falling on the ice. When he fell, he went

Sault Memorial Gardens (bottom of picture),
the home of the Algoma Contractors hockey team.

down like a tree. He didn't know
how to land properly. He fell so often
that his body would get covered with
bruises. The trainer sewed sponges
into Phil's pants to protect his hips,
which got hit the hardest.

But Phil steadily improved. He was great with the stick and became a deadly shot. The Contractors were a powerful team. They didn't often lose a game, but when they did, Phil got very upset. His whole body and mind were wrapped up in playing hockey and winning.

By the time Phil was seventeen years old he felt he was ready to play for a junior-league team. The junior teams were minor-league farm teams that belonged to the pro teams. Playing for the juniors was the only way of getting on a pro team.

Phil tried out for the Chicago Black Hawks Junior A team. Once again he flunked a tryout. But the Hawks offered him a job playing for their Junior B club, the Sarnia Legionnaires.

Sarnia was 350 miles from the Soo. Phil was eager to leave home and give it a try, but his father had some doubts.

"If you're not good enough to play Junior A, you should stay home and forget it," said Pat Esposito.

It was Coach Bombacco who talked Mr. Esposito into letting Phil leave home.

At Sarnia Phil lived with other young hockey players in a rooming house run by a lady the boys affec-

Ma Dagg and her granddaughter.

tionately called Ma Dagg. Mrs. Dagg
took good care of the boys. She woke
them up at eight in the morning and
fed them a good breakfast. Then she

18

sent them off to high school. After school they did their homework. They had hockey practice at night. It was a busy life. There wasn't much time to be homesick.

The boys got paid $27.50 a week. They paid $17.50 for their room and meals. That left $10 a week for spending money.

Mrs. Dagg's home in Sarnia, Ontario.

The dining room where Ma Dagg and the boys ate dinner every night. Phil always sat at the head of the table.

After he was at Sarnia for a while, Phil dropped out of high school. He wanted to spend all his time playing hockey. He decided if he made it in hockey, education wouldn't matter. If he didn't make it, he would drive a truck. Either way, he figured, he didn't need a high school diploma.

Phil's father was furious. He wanted his sons to go to college. He almost pulled Phil out of Sarnia. Once more Coach Bombacco came to Phil's aid.

"You might as well let Phil do what he wants," the coach advised. Mr. Esposito reluctantly agreed.

By Christmas Phil was the leading scorer in the league. The next year he moved to St. Catherines, Ontario, to play for the Hawks Junior A team, the St. Catherines TeePees.

Phil felt as if he were finally getting somewhere. He was earning $57.50 a week in spending money and was one step away from the pros.

At the end of the season Phil was offered a chance to play in a series of three pro grames. But before the series began, he broke his wrist. The games were important ones. The stands would be filled with big-shot Black Hawk officials. Phil had to decide whether or not to play with his broken wrist.

His parents and family doctor were against it. Phil decided to ask the advice of the Hawks chief scout, Bob Wilson.

"If you want to play, then play. If you're worried about the wrist, then don't," Mr. Wilson told him.

Phil decided to play, but his cast was so big he couldn't get his glove on over it. All players had to wear gloves.

Before the first game Phil was at home. He went down in the basement and found a file. He hid behind the furnace because he didn't want his father to see what he was doing. He was scared and sweating as he began to file the cast down.

I've got to make this thing work, Phil thought. *I don't want to wind up driving a truck for the steel mill. I've got to be a pro.*

Phil played, but it almost cost him his career. More damage was done to his wrist during the three games. It hurt him all summer long. The bones were so badly injured that it took a long time for them to go together right. But finally the wrist healed.

''You're a lucky boy,'' the doctor told him.

Phil wished his career had not depended on luck. He was only a teenager. He wished somebody on the Black Hawks Club had cared enough to say, "Look, kid, don't worry about it. Don't take chances with that broken wrist. You've still got a job with us."

Phil was fat and out of shape when he tried
out for the Black Hawks team and often fell
down.

3

Playing for the Black Hawks

Phil was not in good shape when he arrived at the Chicago training camp in the fall of 1962. His injured hand had kept him from working out during the summer. He was fat from lack of exercise. He moved slowly on the ice.

Phil had to settle for the small salary of $3,800. Tom Ivan, the manager of the Hawks, decided Esposito was not ready to play for the Hawks. He sent Phil to play for a farm club in St. Louis for a year.

Phil put in a good year in St. Louis. He scored 35 goals during the season and enjoyed living in St. Louis. The young players on the team were not much interested in saving money. They went out every night and spent all their earnings. Phil also spent a lot of his time with his girlfriend, Linda.

By the end of the season Phil was broke. Phil wanted to get married, but he didn't have enough money to take care of a wife. So Phil drove a truck in the Soo all summer, and he saved every penny. Phil and Linda were married in August.

The next season Phil moved up to the Black Hawks team. He still wasn't making much money, but he was excited. At last he was going to play for the pros.

Phil was so nervous on the airplane trip to Chicago that he couldn't eat. He thought he might get sick.

Wow! I'm going to meet Bobby Hull! he thought with a fluttering feeling in his stomach.

He felt better when he got his uniform with the number 7 on the back. It was the same number he had worn as a boy. Phil put on his uniform and went out into the arena. Bobby Hull came over to shake hands.

When it was time to warm up for the game, Phil felt like a big deal. He skated in circles near Hull. He heard people in the stands asking for his name.

Phil felt a lot worse at the end of the game. Coach Billy Reay had let him play for only three minutes. Phil was scared, and he really didn't have enough time to warm up and get moving.

Phil spent most of his first season with the Hawks on the bench. He hated it. The thrill of making the team soon wore off. He wanted to play. When he did get on the ice, it

Phil Esposito (7) and Bubby Hull (9) try to
get the puck away from Bruins star Bobby Orr.

was for only a few minutes. He tried
so hard to impress the coach in ninety
seconds that he made silly mistakes.

But Phil did not give up. He finally
showed Coach Reay that he was an
expert stickhandler and good at
face-offs and scoring goals. By his
second season Phil was the first
string center.

Phil played for the Black Hawks for four years. He steadily improved and became one of the finest centers in hockey. At the end of the 1965 season the Black Hawks captured first place in the Eastern Division of the National Hockey League for the first time.

Then came one of the biggest shocks in Phil's life. After the winning season he was traded to the struggling Boston Bruins. Phil felt rejected, and he certainly didn't like going from a first-place club to a last-place team.

Phil was depressed when he went back to the Soo for the summer with his family. Pat Esposito tried to cheer up his son.

"What's the matter?" Mr. Esposito asked. "Are you afraid of a little hard work?"

"Of course not," Phil answered.

"Listen," said Pat Esposito. "You are good enough to make it anywhere. Just go out and show them what you can do."

By the end of the summer Phil felt better. The talks with his father had helped. He was determined to play his best for Boston.

"I'm going to show the whole hockey world who Phil Esposito is," he said to himself.

Phil scores against the Toronto Maple Leafs.

4

Traded to the Bruins

Phil found it was much better play-ing for a team where he was really needed. Coach Harry Sinden made Phil an alternate captain. He would have a chance to be a real team leader.

In Chicago Esposito had passed the puck to Bobby Hull, who did most of the scoring. In Boston Phil did a lot of the scoring himself. In his second home game he scored four goals. After the game his father called him on the telephone.

"You see," he said. "There's nothing to it!"

Pat Esposito was right. Phil and the Bruins had a great season. Phil scored 35 goals. He was the second-highest scorer in the league.

The Bruins finished in third place in the NHL's Eastern Division. They were defeated by Montreal in the Stanley Cup play-offs. But they knew they had the makings of a great team. Esposito and Bobby Orr worked perfectly together. Phil would stand near the goal. If Bobby could not get close enough, he would pass to Phil, or if he missed a shot,

Phil would knock it in. Hodge, Stan-
field, Green, and a rookie named
Derek Sanderson were also rising
stars on the team.

Esposito scores again!

The Bruins were a tough, hard-working team, but they also liked to have a good time. There was a lot of joking and fooling around during practice and in the dressing rooms. The rest of the team teased Phil about his many superstitions.

Before every game, when Phil walked into the dressing room, he would always wink at a red horn hanging over his seat. His grandmother had given him the horn to ward off the "evil eye." Under his jersey Phil would put on a tattered black good-luck T-shirt, making sure it was inside out and backward. He would pin a St. Christopher medal to his suspenders. Then he would put on the rest of his clothes right to left.

"I dress right to left," he explained. "I put my right sock on first, then my left. Then everything else, right first, then left."

Phil also warned his teammates not to cross their hockey sticks in the dressing room.

"See a crossed stick in the dressing room, and you lose," he said.

Sanderson and Esposito became a two-man comedy act on the long bus rides between games. They also liked to sing.

"One night on the bus we sang for two and a half hours," recalls San-

The Esposito-Sanderson comedy team.

derson. "We sang everything from Bob Dylan to the Beatles. Naturally, Espie sang every Italian song he knew."

There were some sportswriters

who thought Esposito's first high-scoring season with Boston was pure luck. They said he would never do as well again.

The Bruins set out to prove the sportswriters wrong in the 1968–69 season. Coach Sinden had Phil centering for Hodge and Ron Murphy. No one could stop the three forwards. The trio scored the most points ever made by a line in pro hockey—263. Points are earned not only by scoring goals, but also by helping another player score a goal. The Bruins finished in second place in their league.

Phil also broke a pro hockey scoring record by piling up an amazing

total of 126 points. No player had
ever even got 100 points before.

Phil's teammates congratulate him after he be-
comes the first hockey player to score 100
points in one season.

Experts studied Esposito's style. They could see that when he had the puck, he ruled the game. He had a fantastic ability to slow the game down to a scoring pace. Many forwards miss goals because they are moving too fast.

Goaltenders marveled at the variety and speed of Phil's shots. They were completely baffled by them.

"When Phil gets that puck in front of the cage," said goalie Gerry Desjardins, "he is all arms and legs and looks twelve feet wide. He doesn't get excited and rush the shot. He gets you down on the ice, and then the game is over. Phil's very accurate at aiming into corners."

Phil gives his daughter Laurie, his sister
Teresa, and a neighbor boy a ride in the snow
outside his Boston home.

5

World Champions

In the 1969–70 season Phil scored
a league-leading 43 goals. Boston
and Chicago finished in a tie for first
place in the Eastern Division of the
NHL. But the Black Hawks were
awarded first place because they had
scored more goals than the Bruins.

Phil was pleased with his record,
but he still wanted two things—first
place in his division and a Stanley
Cup victory.

After the regular hockey season is over, the leading teams in the Eastern and Western divisions of the NHL play each other in the Stanley Cup series. The winner of the series is named the best professional hockey team in the world.

There are three rounds in the Stanley Cup play-offs. The winner of each round is the first team to win four games.

The Bruins had been in the Stanley Cup play-offs before, but they had never won it. They were determined that the 1970 series would be different.

The opening round was against the Bruins' old rivals, the New York

Esposito jumps for joy after he scores three
goals in one game against the Rangers.

Rangers. The series began at Boston
Garden. Phil was the star of the
game. He scored 3 goals and led his
team to an easy 8 to 2 victory. The
Bruins also won the second game by
a score of 5 to 3.

Leading the series two games to none, the Bruins flew to New York for the next two games to be held at Madison Square Garden. Because of the fierce competition between the two teams, tempers were ready to flare as the players skated into the arena. After only a minute of play a full-scale war broke out on the ice. A couple of Rangers hit Derek Sanderson. Seeing their teammate in trouble, the whole Bruin team flooded into the arena, swinging their sticks and their fists. It took the referees several minutes to break up the fight and start the game again. The penalty boxes were so full they looked like

players' benches. The Rangers went
on to win. They won the next game,
too.

Phil (third from left) and teammates look out
sadly from the penalty box.

When the two teams flew back to Boston, the series was tied two games to two. The Rangers kept up the pressure. Early in the fifth game they went ahead by a score of 2 to 1. Then Esposito took charge. He scored two goals in a row. Boston won by a score of 3 to 2. The Bruins had put an end to the Rangers' winning streak.

The final game was played in New York. Boston won easily. The Bruins were now ready for the second Stanley Cup round, in which they would face the team that had robbed them of first place—the Chicago Black Hawks.

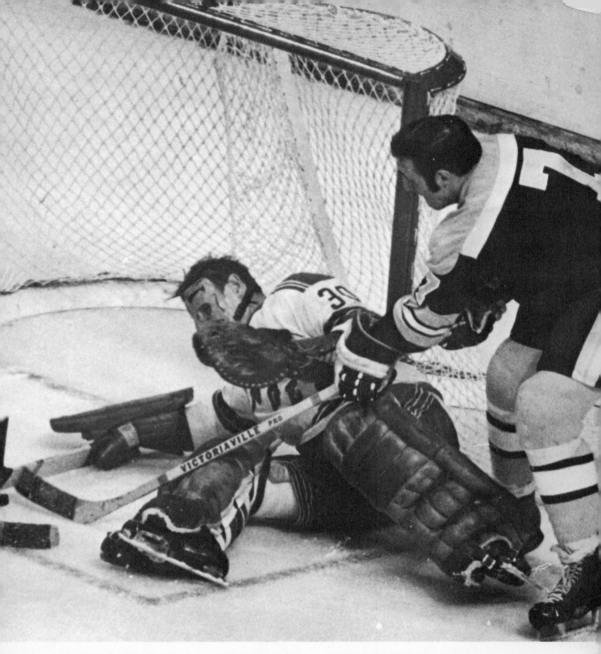

Esposito knocks down Ranger goalie Terry Saw-
chuk to score.

Phil was particularly anxious to beat the Hawks. He was still angry about the way the Chicago team had treated him. There was another reason, too. Phil's brother, Tony, was the superstar goalie for the Hawks. The two brothers were good friends, but they had also grown up competing with each other.

The series opened in Chicago, and all the hockey world wondered which brother would win the battle of the Espositos. In the first few seconds of the game Bruins forward Ken Hodge knocked Tony to the ice with a hard shot that hit the goalie just behind his mask, near his temple.

"Tony went down like a ton of bricks," Phil said later. "I was scared to death. I just skated around in little circles. I wanted to go help my brother. I could see everybody crowding around him, and him laying there on the ice out cold. It was awful. Then that fine gentleman Bobby Hull came down the ice and skated past me, and as he did he said, 'Don't worry, Phil, he's OK.' He knew how close Tony and I were."

Once Tony was up again, Boston really went to work on the Hawks. They won by a score of 6 to 3. Three of the Bruin goals were scored by Phil Esposito.

"He was gangbusters tonight," Tony said after the game. "Bang. Bang. Bang. He was always in the right place at the right time. He could have scored three more goals."

In the rest of the series Phil scored twice more. Boston won in four straight games.

Now there was no stopping the Bruins. In the third round of the play-offs they demolished the St. Louis Blues by winning four in a row.

Phil and the Bruins had achieved one of their goals. They were world champions.

Phil was also becoming a success

off the ice. He teamed up with a friend named Fred Sharf, who ran a small sporting goods business. The two business partners visited many factories that made hockey equipment. Phil discovered that the quality of the sticks made for boys was poor. They were usually adult sticks with the ends sawed off. They didn't have the right balance for a boy. Smaller sticks were merely toys and broke easily.

Phil had a sturdy stick made that was the right size for boys. It had a fiberglass-faced blade. He also designed gloves, shin guards, and all sorts of protective equipment. Soon a

Businessman Phil Esposito discusses an ad for
his street hockey equipment.

full line of Phil Esposito products was ready to be sold. No hockey player had ever put out a complete line of gear before. Phil called his company Phil Esposito Enterprises.

Phil (7) goes for the puck in an opening face-off.

6

Finishing First and Winning
the Stanley Cup

It was going to be tough for the Bruins to improve on their 1969–70 championship season. After winning the Stanley Cup, Harry Sinden had resigned as Boston's coach. The club's assistant manager, Tom Johnson, took over for him.

Johnson had Esposito centering for Ken Hodge, his old friend from Black Hawk days, and Wayne

Cushman, who was one of the league's best fighters.

The three forwards worked together like a well-oiled machine. They also made an impressive sight because they were the biggest line in pro hockey. Phil stood 6 feet 1 inch tall and weighed 205 pounds. Hodge was 6 feet 2 and weighed 212 pounds. Cushman was 6 feet 1 and weighed 192 pounds.

Phil was in perfect condition. In the first two months of the 1970–71 season he skated as if he owned the ice. On March 12, 1971, he broke Bobby Hull's record for scoring the most goals in one season. Phil

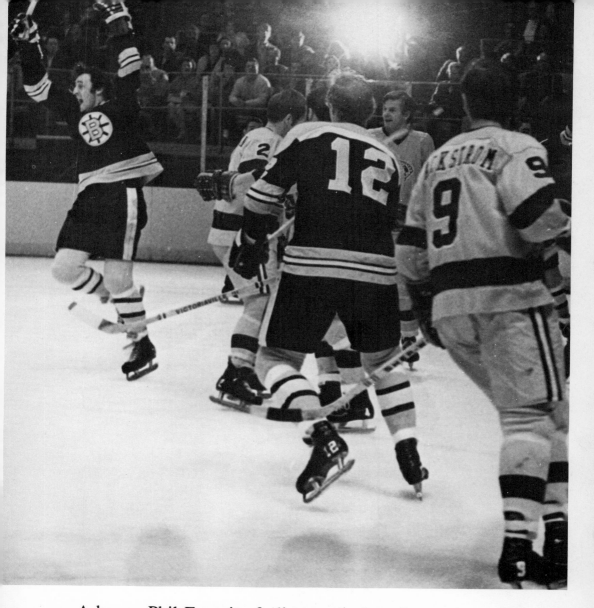

A happy Phil Esposito frolics on the ice after he has just become the first player in the history of hockey to score more than 58 goals in one season.

finished the season with 76 goals; Hull's record had been 58.

The Bruins finished the season in first place in the Eastern Division with the greatest record in hockey history. They were favored to win the Stanley Cup again. But they didn't. Boston was overconfident, and the

The Bruins are bitterly disappointed when they lose the Stanley Cup.

Montreal Canadiens knocked them out of the series in the first round. After such a spectacular season, the loss was a big letdown for the Bruins.

Beginning the 1971–72 season, it was clear to the Bruins what they had to do. They had to finish first and win the Stanley Cup. Montreal was no longer a threat because they had lost some of their best players. The team most likely to keep them from their goal was the Bruins' old enemy, the New York Rangers.

In the opening game of the season between the two teams New York beat Boston by a score of 4 to 1. The loss was good for the Bruins. It made them furious at the Rangers. Boston won the next five games in which the two clubs played.

With each loss the New York fans showed their increasing dislike for the Boston team. They yelled names and threw garbage at the Bruins whenever they visited Madison Square Garden.

But the Bruins kept on winning. At the end of the season they were in first place. The New York Rangers were a distant second.

The cry went up all over Boston: "ON TO THE CUP!"

In the first round of the Stanley Cup series the Bruins beat the Toronto Maple Leafs in five games. Then they took the St. Louis Blues in

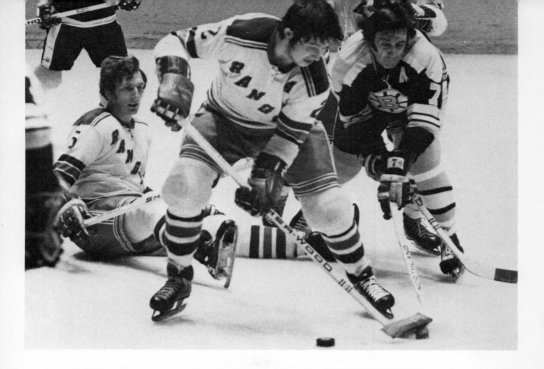

Phil tries to grab the puck from Ranger Brad Park.

four straight games. In the final round they met the New York Rangers.

The Rangers' plan was to put one of their strongest players, Walter Tkaczuk, to work guarding Esposito. That was all right with Phil. Keeping

Tkaczuk busy would give the other Bruins a better chance to score.

The Bruins won the first two games of the series in Boston. Phil didn't score, but he earned several points making assists. He was play-ing well, considering how closely he was being guarded.

The powerful Esposito fights to get in close to the net to wait for a pass.

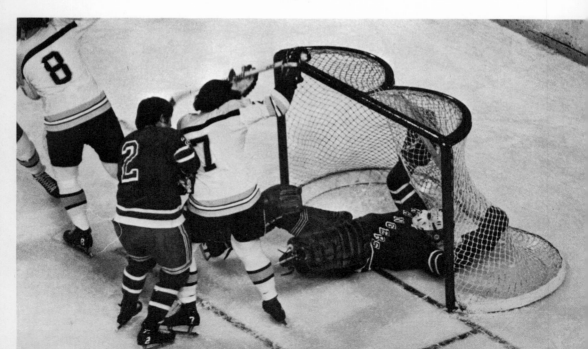

The third game was played in New York. Phil looked up into the stands, where the fans were screaming and holding up signs. One read: YOU'RE A DISGRACE TO THE ITALIANS. Another said: SPAGHETTI HEAD. The Bruins lost the third game. But they won the fourth and went back to Boston leading the series three games to one.

A win in Boston would end the series. The Bruins were confident, but it didn't work out the way they hoped. They were defeated by two goals. Both teams went back to New York for the sixth game.

In front of New York's howling

fans the Bruins won the Stanley Cup by defeating the Rangers by a score of 3 to 0. The Boston club accepted the cup and left the ice quickly. Ranger fans were throwing things at them.

There was a celebration in the clubhouse after the game. The players passed around the gold Stanley Cup.

At one in the morning the tired Bruins boarded their charter flight back to Boston. They laughed and joked during the flight. They had good reason to be happy. At long last they were first in their division and the proud owners of the Stanley Cup.

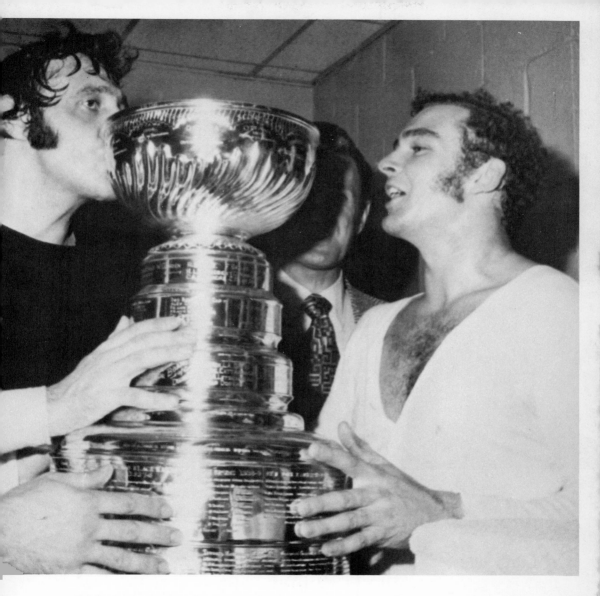

Phil kisses the Stanley Cup as teammate Ken
Hodge looks on following the Bruins' win over
the Rangers.

Orr and Esposito grimly push through crowds
of enthusiastic fans.

When the plane touched down at
Logan Airport in Boston, what
should have been a joyful homecom-

ing turned into a nightmare. More than 10,000 people had shown up to welcome the champions. The Bruin players had to run for their cars to keep from being trampled by the enthusiastic fans.

The next day Mayor Kevin White invited the team to City Hall for a reception and lunch. Phil and a few other players went out onto a balcony overlooking a large public square. An enormous crowd had gathered below waiting to catch a glimpse of the Stanley Cup champions. Phil smiled and waved. Thousands of fans waved back. Right then it felt pretty good being Phil Esposito.

Bruins superstar, Phil Esposito.

7

Team Canada vs. the Russians

In spite of breaking scoring rec-
ords year after year Phil Esposito
was never as much of a hero to hockey fans as Bobby Orr, Gordie
Howe, or Bobby Hull. Some fans
complained that all he did was knock
in Bobby Orr's rebounds and that
anybody who skated in such a plod-
ding manner could not be called a
great hockey player.

But in the fall of 1972 an event took place that made the whole hockey world see that Phil Esposito was one of the game's all-time great players. The best hockey players in Canada were to meet the best players from the Soviet Union in a series of eight games.

The series was more than just an exhibition. It was a battle between two countries. The honor of Canada, the birthplace of ice hockey, was at stake. Professional NHL stars who long had bragged that they were the best in the world would, for the first time, play against the best skaters ever seen in Europe.

In 1972 ice hockey was the number one sport in the Soviet Union. Hockey arenas everywhere were jammed. Millions more fans watched the game on TV.

Harry Sinden, who had coached the Boston Bruins to the Stanley Cup in 1970, was appointed head coach of the NHL squad, named Team Canada. He invited the best players in the NHL to play for Canada.

Unfortunately, two of Canada's best players would not be in the lineup. Bobby Hull no longer played for the NHL, so he was not allowed to play. Bobby Orr was out because he had just had surgery on his knee.

The Russians had an unfair advantage. The Soviet team played together ten months out of the year. The Canadian team was made up from players from different NHL teams. Team Canada played together for the first time two and a half weeks before the series began. The players were not used to working together. Still the Canadians were confident. After all, ice hockey was Canada's game.

People who watched the Russians practice were impressed most with the stamina of the players. They skated and skated without ever getting tired. No one wiped his face with

Team Canada's coach Harry Sinden answers questions at a press conference. Looking on are Bobby Orr, Phil Esposito, Tony Esposito, and assistant coach John Ferguson.

a towel after a hard skate. No one bent over to catch his breath. No one sneaked a drink.

On the day of the first game in Montreal Phil was more nervous than before any other game. But he won the opening face-off, and thirty seconds later Team Canada scored. Six minutes later the Canadians scored again.

Still Phil had a funny feeling that the Russians would be a difficult team to beat. The Soviet team was losing 2 to 0 on strange ice in a foreign country, but they looked as fresh as when the game began. Montreal was suffering from a heat wave. It was 90 degrees in the arena, but the heat didn't seem to bother the Russian players.

Soon Phil's fears came true. The Russians tied the game as the Canadians began to tire. They went ahead to win by a score of 7 to 3.

All Canada was crushed by the defeat. Out of a population of 22,000,000, 16,000,000 had watched the game on TV. No other sporting event had ever attracted so much attention. The players were roaring mad. They wanted their honor back.

The Canadians managed to win the second game, but they only tied the

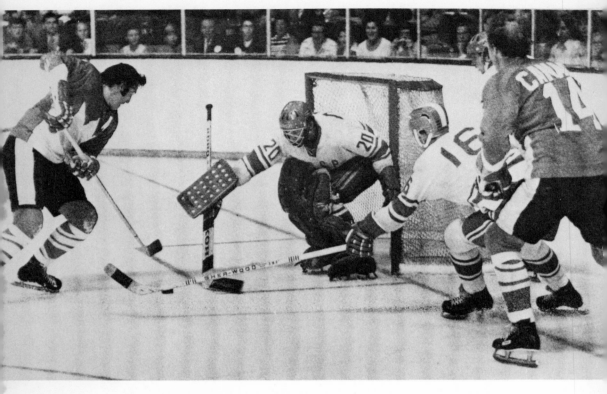

Phil scores in the second game of Team Canada's series against the Russians.

third game and lost the fourth and final game played in Canada.

The fans couldn't believe it. They jeered at the Canadian players as they drove through the streets of Vancouver after the fourth game.

The Canadian players were upset and angry about losing, but what bothered them most was the reaction of the fans. After the fourth game Phil told millions of fans on national TV how discouraged the players were at being ridiculed by their own countrymen. He told them that he admired the Russians' skill, but that he and the other players were doing their best. He spoke with passion and even anger.

After the broadcast the station was flooded with phone calls and telegrams supporting the Canadians. Phil and his teammates felt better. But they had yet to prove they were the best players in the world.

On to Moscow, where by now Phil was the unquestioned leader of the team. He never let up. In the four games there Phil not only led scoring, but killed penalties, ran the power plays, fought anybody who got in his way, and shouted and waved angrily at the crowds when they annoyed him. He did all this in an atmosphere that would have frightened most men. The rink was filled with armed and uniformed Russians.

At first the Soviet fans were quiet and well behaved. The 3,000 Canadian fans who had traveled to the

Soviet Union for the series were not so restrained. They rang cowbells and waved banners, blew horns and chanted for goals. As the series went on, the Soviet fans began to whistle to drown out the Canadian cheers and chants. Tension mounted throughout the big ice palace.

Led by the determined Esposito, the Canadians won the first three games of the series. The final game set a new peak in excitement. More than 15,000 fans jammed into the arena with only 13,000 seats. They clogged every aisle and threatened to spill out onto the ice itself. The noise made by the now totally out-of-control fans was almost unbearable. The Russians got ahead by a score of 5 to 3 by the end of the second period. It looked as if they couldn't be stopped.

But then Phil took charge. Early in the third period he fought off the Russians in front of the net and banged in a goal to make it 5 to 4. Then he threw a pass for the goal that tied up the game.

The tide had turned, but wait! When the tying puck had gone in, the light in back of the net hadn't gone on. Alan Eagleson, who was the lawyer and good friend of many of the Canadians, got so angry that he stormed out onto the ice in a towering rage. Within seconds, half a dozen armed and uniformed Russians in tan greatcoats and hats were carrying the struggling Eagleson out of the arena.

Esposito and Frank Mahovlich leaped off the bench and led a pack of Canadian players to Eagleson's side. With their sticks waving high in the air, they wrestled the lawyer clear and escorted him, slipping and sliding, back across the ice to their bench. The tying score appeared on the scoreboards.

To restore order, two long lines of soldiers marched into the arena and completely circled the ice surface. A

Team Canada's Phil Esposito raises his stick
in victory as the winning goal is scored by
teammate Paul Henderson.

tense quiet settled over the ice palace. For ten minutes the two teams roared up and down the ice with nobody scoring. With less than a minute to go the tireless Esposito grabbed the puck from the Russians and shot. The Russian goalie blocked his shot, but teammate Paul Henderson put it in for the winning goal.

Team Canada had won back its honor by winning four games in a row on Russian soil, and Phil Esposito was a national hero.

The star of the eight-game Canada-Russia series speaks to a crowd of 80,000 fans who have
waited for hours in pouring rain to welcome
Team Canada home.

8

Building a New Team

When Phil returned to North America as a conquering hero, he had to face more problems. Something new had been added to the hockey scene. A brand-new league had been formed—the World Hockey Association. The WHA was offering big money to tempt National Hockey League stars.

The first to change leagues was Esposito's Chicago friend, Bobby

Hull, who signed a multimillion-dollar contract with the WHA's Winnipeg Jets. Once Hull made the jump, other NHL stars followed.

The Bruins were hit the hardest. Goalie Gerry Cheevers signed with the Cleveland Crusaders. Derek Sanderson became the highest-paid hockey player in the world when he moved to the Philadelphia Blazers. Johnny McKenzie, Ted Green, Ed Westfall, and Dan Bouchard also left to join WHA teams.

Phil had mixed feelings. He was glad to see his teammates happy and making so much money. But he was sad to see his friends go. And he knew that the Bruins would have to start all over again to build a winning team. Still, he was sure it could be done.

The Bruins had a rough time as they began the 1972–73 season. They lost their first game with the Rangers by a score of 7 to 1. With so many of the old players gone, the Bruins had lost their touch.

The only thing that was not missing was Esposito's determination and deadly shooting. He picked up right where he left off and climbed right to the top of the scoring race.

But Phil was not able to do it all alone. The Bruins kept losing, and the owners of the Boston club decided something had to be done.

Harry Sinden, the Bruins' old coach and leader of Team Canada, was brought in to make the changes.

Armand Guidolin replaced Tom Johnson as head coach. Derek Sanderson was bought back from Philadelphia. The Bruins traded to get the Maple Leafs' goaltender, Jacques Plante. Bobby Orr got better and was back on the ice.

The changes worked. It was not long before the Bruins were a winning team again, and they climbed to second place by the end of the season. But when they met the New York Rangers in the first round of the Stanley Cup play-offs, something happened to the Bruins' magic. The

Rangers won the opening game by a score of 6 to 2.

In the second game Phil was skating across the center line when he was hit hard by three Rangers, one from behind and two in front. A crunch was heard all around Boston Garden.

Phil falls to the ice, gripping his injured right knee.

Phil crumpled to the ice, his right cheek pressed painfully against the cold ice. He had felt something snap in his knee. As he was carried out on a stretcher, Phil still held his stick firmly in his hand.

He was rushed to the hospital, where doctors told Phil he had some badly torn ligaments in his knee. He was through for the season, and so were the Bruins.

When the 1973–74 season began, Esposito was back in the lineup. The Bruins were as hot as ever. They ended up first in their division and were the predicted Stanley Cup winners.

The Bruins breezed through the first two rounds and met a new team to the league, the Philadelphia Flyers, for the final round. To the amazement of hockey fans everywhere, the fledgling team toppled the mighty Bruins in a close series. After tying the series three games to three, the Flyers won the cup in the seventh game.

But Phil Esposito's determination to be the best didn't leave him. As usual, he looked ahead, not back.

"There's always next year," said the big man who has shattered every scoring record in the game and is one of the world's finest hockey players.

The Authors

MARSHALL BURCHARD, a former education editor of *Time* magazine, is presently a free-lance writer. SUE BURCHARD, a librarian at Trinity School, also writes on a free-lance basis. The Burchards have previously co-authored *Sports Hero* biographies of Joe Namath, Brooks Robinson, Kareem Abdul Jabbar, Johnny Bench, Bobby Orr, Roger Staubach, Henry Aaron, Billie Jean King, Richard Petty, and Larry Csonka.

DISCARD